Cane and rush
seating

Cane and rush seating

Margery Brown

Larousse and Co., Inc.
New York, New York

© Margery Brown 1976
First published 1976 in the
United States by Larousse and Co., Inc.
572 Fifth Avenue
New York, New York 10036

ISBN 0–88332–044–5 (hardback)
ISBN 0–88332–075–4 (paperback)
Library of Congress Catalog Card Number 76–15023

Printed in Great Britain
Reprinted 1977

Contents

Acknowledgment

I acknowledge with thanks the Edward James Foundation, Mrs O N Boniface, Mrs A Fordham, Mr J C Guy and Mrs Piper for kindly lending seats to be photographed; Mr J W Brown, Mr Peter Stevens of Poole, Dorset, and Mr C Paul Wilson of Emsworth, Hampshire, for supplying photographs; also *Womancraft* magazine for use of material.

Broadstone   **M B** 1976

Introduction

The history of chairs and seats in general is fascinating, and like many other subjects the more one researches, the more there is to learn. The chairs in our homes which we take so much for granted today were, in mediaeval times, very rare indeed. If we study old prints and drawings of the Manor Houses of the period, we will see stools and benches in the great hall which were used for seating the family and servants of the household. There probably would be one chair only, made in very heavy oak, rather like a small bench or chest, with a straight back and sometimes arms added. This would be reserved for the master of the house, or his most important guest. This fact may be the origin of the term 'taking the chair' or 'chairing the meeting'. Chairs were few in the reign of Queen Elizabeth I, and were still made of heavy oak, though with a little more variety in style, and a little more thought for comfort. This trend continued during the following reign and the Commonwealth.

France was far ahead of England at this time. French craftsmen were advanced in skill and technique and were experimenting with many different woods and materials. When Charles II returned from France, after his restoration to the throne, he brought with him the newer ideas and fashions. The whole trend was away from the dark, heavy furniture which had been in use so long, to lighter, more stylish shapes, using many different kinds of wood, including beech and walnut. With these lighter woods a great deal of caning became fashionable, for chair seats, backs, bedheads and tables, and this new style of furniture became very popular.

In the eighteenth century came the great names of furniture designers, of whom Chippendale was one of the most famous. He designed some of the most elegant and graceful furniture ever made. His chairs were shaped for comfort, and made with splendid carving on the backs and legs, often with an acanthus leaf design which he used a great deal in his work.

Heppelwhite, who followed him, continued the trend for gayer and more delicate furniture, using inlays of varying coloured woods to decorate his work. His chairs were often designed with shield shaped backs. Sheraton at this time was designing plainer chairs, with a great deal of caning for seats and backs.

At the present time, chairs of all shapes and sizes are an integral part of our home furnishings. A great many people have beautiful old chairs which are in need of reseating and they have difficulty in finding anyone capable of doing the work.

This book is written in the hope that it may be helpful and encouraging to the many students who have attended my classes in these crafts, and who wish to continue practising the different techniques of seating. Also I hope it will introduce the craft to those who have not yet attempted it, but may perhaps be inspired to do so. Using natural materials, some of which are grown in Britain, the weaving of strong and attractive seats with rushes, willows or cane can give great pleasure and a real sense of achievement. The techniques generally are traditional and have stood the test of time, but others are modern and provide scope for new designs.

I have included a section on seagrass and cord seating in which a great variety of patterns and styles can be tested by the enthusiastic student who may also wish to experiment with some of the new materials now available.

Cane seating

6 WAY PATTERN

The cane used for chair seating grows in Eastern tropical areas and is called *rattan*. It is a strong plant which produces thorny tendrils to climb over the surrounding vegetation, reaching to great lengths. The inner bark, which has a very hard and glossy surface, is stripped off and cut into varying widths. This is the cane used for chair seating, and the remainder of the rattan, which would be up to 25 mm (1 in.) in diameter, is cut into different thicknesses for use as basketry cane, known as *centre cane* or *pulp cane*.

   The craft of chair caning is not difficult, the main requirements are care and patience. It cannot be hurried as the work is done in stages, each of which must be completed before the next one can be started. The tools required are few and if not readily available can mostly be improvised.

1 Seat in 6 way pattern

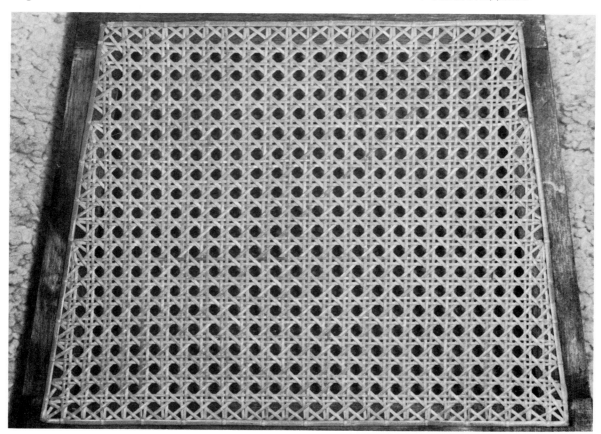

Tools for cane seating

A sharp penknife

A small hammer

Scissors or side cutters

A small stiletto (125–150 mm) (5–6 in.)

A clearing tool
(This is for clearing the old cane from the chair before starting to re-cane.) It is a tool rather like a screwdriver but with a flat top. An old screwdriver with about 38 mm (1½ in.) cut off to leave a flat top, or a small-headed nail about 50 mm (2 in.) long can be used for this purpose.

Pegs
These are small pieces of wood, willow, or centre cane which are used to peg the cane in the holes as you are working, so they are most useful if cut to a point. Incidentally, golf tees make excellent temporary pegs.

In addition to these side cutters, round-nosed and flat-nosed pliers would be useful.

1 Tools for cane seating; *left to right.* Small stiletto; Clearing tool; Curved needle; Side cutters; Flat-nosed pliers; Round-nosed pliers

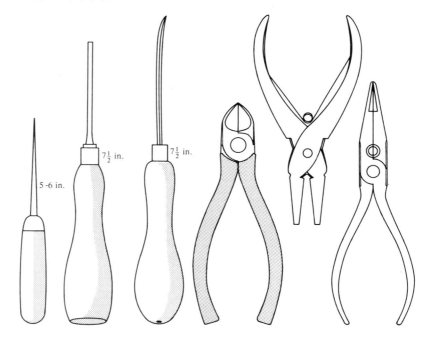

Cane

The sizes of cane in general use are from no. 1 (very narrow) up to no. 6 which is about 6 mm ($\frac{1}{4}$ in.) in width, and is mostly used for covering the holes when the seating is completed. Apart from this, two sizes of cane are usually used for weaving a seat, which in the first pattern I shall give is worked in six stages, plus the edge covering already mentioned.

The first four stages are worked with no. 2 cane, and the last two stages with no. 3 cane. The size of the cane used depends on the spacing of the holes, which you will find varies a great deal in different chairs. On the normal size of bedroom chair the holes will probably be about 13 mm ($\frac{1}{2}$ in.) apart from centre to centre, but sometimes they are much more widely spaced, in which case it would be better to use no. 3 cane for the first four stages, and no. 4 cane for the last two stages. This would strengthen the seat. The glossy side of the cane is, of course, the right side.

It is supplied in 250 gramme ($\frac{1}{2}$ lb) bundles, and if you wish to work on several chairs, this is the most economical way to buy it. Craft shops, however, often supply small bundles which give sufficient of each size for one chair, and this can be most useful.

The cane needs to be dampened before use, but do not damp the whole bundle, just take out a few lengths and put them into cold or tepid water for about two minutes, then wrap them in a towel or piece of blanket for about fifteen minutes. Take out one piece to work with and keep the remainder wrapped until needed.

The first step is to clear the old cane from the seat. With a sharp knife cut round just inside the seat frame so that the whole centre of the seat is removed. Cut away the beading (if any) over the holes and you will probably find that every alternate hole has a little peg in it. With the clearing tool and hammer knock out these pegs. Every hole must be completely cleared of pegs and cane, and if, as sometimes happens, glue has been used in the holes, you may have to drill them out. Also if the seat needs any attention to worm holes or painting, do this before starting on the seating.

When weaving the last three stages, many people like to use the shell bodkin to help thread the canes through. Personally I have never found this necessary. I prefer to do it with my fingers, but this is a matter for personal decision. A tool which I do find very useful, especially when weaving the two diagonal stages, is a small stiletto with which to lift the canes lying on the frame, when trying to thread the diagonal canes underneath them.

As I have said, the 6 way pattern is worked in six stages, the last three of which are woven in different directions, which gives the seat its great strength (see photograph 1). For order of working see pages 82 to 92.

Materials

No. 2 cane for first 4 stages

No. 3 cane for last 2 stages

No. 6 and no. 2 cane for beading and couching if required.

Stage One

Now that the chair is ready, and the cane prepared, you can start work. Mark the centre hole in the back rail of your chair, and the centre hole in the front rail. Should there be an even number of holes and therefore no centre one, mark the two central ones at the back and in the front. Take a long piece of no. 2 cane and draw it down through the marked hole in the back rail to about half its length, and peg it there with a temporary peg. You will now have half the cane on top of the frame and half underneath. Use the top one first and bring it straight forward to the front rail and thread it down through the marked hole and then up through the next hole either to the right or the left, whichever you prefer. (See diagram 2.) When threading the cane through the holes, *always* run it through your fingers first to ensure that the right side is uppermost all the time, both on top and underneath. This is most important to prevent twisting. At the beginning of the work it is easy to straighten the cane in the hole if it does twist, but in later stages it is almost impossible, so you will save yourself a great deal of frustration if you form a good habit to start with.

Take the cane from the front rail to the back, down through the corresponding hole and up the next and forward to the front again. Continue in this way until you have used up that end of cane, then go back to the other end and work that one out in the same way, pegging the ends. Peg each hole as you take the cane through it, so that the cane is held firmly while you go on to the next hole. The pegs can be moved along as you work; the only pegs that should remain in place are the ones holding short ends of cane which are all left underneath the seat. When you need to start a new piece of cane, peg it in the hole in the opposite rail to the one you have just finished, leaving an end of about 76 mm (3 in.) underneath. Continue until all the holes in the back rail have canes in with the exception of the corner holes—these are all left empty until the fifth stage. You will probably find that you have a few extra holes in the front rail; these are completed as shown in diagram 3. Remember to keep the right side of the cane showing on the top of the seat, and also where it passes from one hole to another underneath. It is easy to achieve this by giving it a half turn in the hole. Do not pull the cane too tightly as you will have to do some weaving in the later stages, so you need a little play in the first stages.

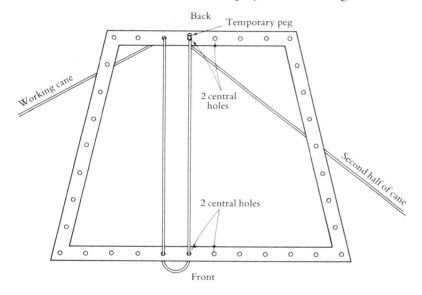

2 6 way pattern, commencing first stage

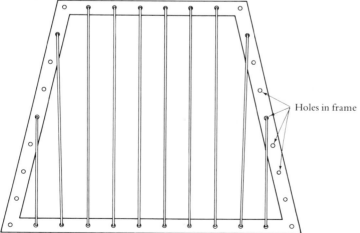

3 6 way pattern, first stage, showing how cane is threaded on a shaped seat (corners left open)

Stage two

The second stage is worked in exactly the same way as the first, but taking the cane from one side rail to the other, on top of the first stage canes, and still leaving the corner holes empty.

Stage three

The third stage repeats the first one, but working over stage two. As you work, try to move your first cane slightly to the left so that the new one will lie to the right of it, and not directly on top. This will make stage four much simpler, as the canes will be correctly placed for weaving. These first three stages really act as a kind of warp for the three weaving stages.

Stage four

Great care must be taken to get this stage correct or the diagonal weaves will not work out as they should. Starting at the right hand side rail, peg a new piece of cane into the first hole from the corner in the front, and weave it over the first and under the second cane of each pair of vertical canes. This is worked below (ie to the front of) the cane of stage two. The best way of working this is to have one hand on top of the seat and the other hand underneath, and using a short end of the new cane, feed it from one hand to the other, over and under the correct canes. Do this over four or five of your vertical pairs (not more) and then carefully pull the cane through. Do not try to pull the cane through right across the seat in one operation, or you may break the vertical canes. Work each row in this way so that the canes form a darning weave.

There are now two diagonal stages to be woven, one from right to left, and the second from left to right, and these should be woven with no. 3 cane.

Stage five (first diagonal) no. 3 cane

Starting in the back right hand corner hole, peg your piece of cane, leaving 76 mm (3 in.) below the seat, and after running the length through your fingers, take it to the left over the first pair of vertical canes, and then straight forward under the horizontal pair, then again to the left over the second vertical pair and again forward under the second horizontal pair. Continue this movement across to the left hand rail. This is where the cane will twist if you give it the slightest opportunity so work very carefully as recommended in stage four, working over and under about four pairs of canes with a short end, and pulling it straight down and up again from one hand to the other, without allowing any loops to form, then with your right hand holding the long loop close to the seat, pull through gently with the left hand. The cane will probably not come out at the corner on the left rail—this will depend on the shape and size of the seat—but it should be threaded down whichever hole it reaches after forming a true diagonal, either on the left rail or the front. Bring the cane up through the adjacent hole and work across to the right hand side again in exactly the same way as the previous strand, and running parallel with it. As this is the first time you have used the corner holes, please note that all the other holes have two canes in, and you must now get two strands in each corner hole. (See diagram 4.) It is important not to miss any holes in the back or the front rails, but if the shape of the seat necessitates any adjustment of the pattern it should be made on the side rails, either by putting two canes into one hole or by missing a hole as necessary.

On the ordinary type of bedroom chair there are usually two holes to be missed on one side, and two holes having two canes in, on the other side. Continue following this diagonal right across the seat. The final strands at the corners will go across the corners if you have worked it correctly.

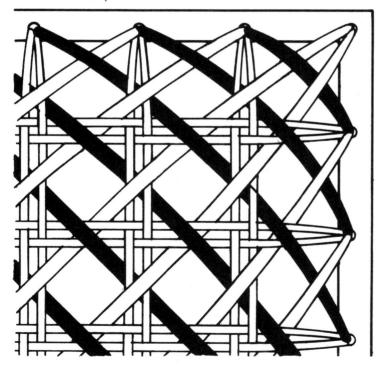

4 6 way pattern. Details of diagonals at corner

2 Chair seat showing pegged finish. 6 way pattern

Stage six (second diagonal)

This is worked from the back left hand corner to the front right hand corner as stage five but reversing all you did in that stage. Where you went over the vertical canes you must now go under them and over the horizontal ones. The adjustments on the side rails are also reversed—where you missed holes in the first diagonal you must now put in double canes, and where you had double canes, you must now miss the holes (see photographs 1 and 3). If you study the diagrams carefully you will see how the diagonals are actually worked and how they run in the little grooves formed by the first four stages, and also how the adjustments on the side rails work out. In diagram 6 you can see the right and wrong way of working—(A) is correct, and (B) is wrong as you can see; the canes are cutting against each other at every crossing, and this will cause the seat to wear out very quickly.

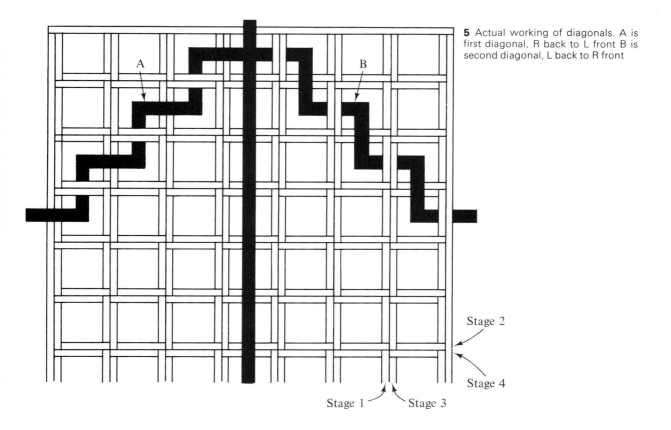

5 Actual working of diagonals. A is first diagonal, R back to L front B is second diagonal, L back to R front

A

B

Stage 2

Stage 4

Stage 1   Stage 3

If when you come to weave stage four, you find that owing to the shape of the seat, or the spacing of the holes, it is difficult to weave in front of the second stage, it would be in order to weave behind (ie at the back of) the cane of stage two as long as every row is done in the same way, making each row alternate. The other change you must then make is to alter your diagonal weaves. Stage five will start in the right hand back corner as given in the instructions, but must go *under* the vertical canes and *over* the horizontal canes, and stage six will start in the left back corner and weave *over* the vertical pairs and *under* the horizontal ones, thus ensuring that the diagonals are still running in their little grooves. (See diagram 6.)

6 Right and wrong way of working diagonals. A is correct, B is wrong (see text)

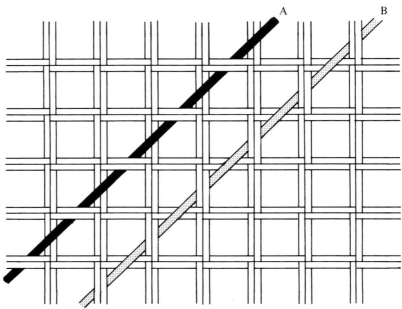

Finishing

There are two ways of completing the seat.

The first is by pegging every hole with a permanent peg—antique chairs were often finished in this way. You will need pegs cut a little shorter than the depth of the rail, so that they do not poke out underneath. They should be very tight fitting in order to keep all the canes firmly held. Put the peg into the hole, hammer it in lightly, and then with the clearing tool on it hammer it right in just below the surface of the rail. Never hammer directly on to the seat as you may damage the polish and break the canes. When every hole has been pegged in this way, cut off all the ends of cane closely underneath, and your seat is complete (see photograph 2).

The second way of finishing is by putting on a beading of wider cane to cover the holes. In this case every alternate hole, counting from each corner, is pegged. The corner holes are all left open for the present. When checking which holes will be pegged and which will be open, if you find that you have an even number of holes and therefore cannot make them alternate, always count from the corners, so that if you must have two pegs together or two open holes, they will come in the centre of the rail. Mark the holes which are to be pegged on each rail, still leaving the corners open. All the ends of cane now left underneath the seat must go into holes that are to be pegged. Those that are in non-peg holes must be threaded up to the top of the seat through the adjacent hole which *will* be pegged. When these are threaded up all round the seat you will have some ends on top and some underneath, so proceed to peg these holes securely as in the first method. Make sure that the canes threaded up to the top do not push down into loops when you put in your pegs. When all are firmly pegged, cut off all the ends closely both on top and underneath. You will now have an open hole between each peg, and the corners will also be open.

Take four short lengths of beading cane (no. 6) each a little longer than one of the rails of the chair, and a long length of no. 2 cane with which to do the couching. This is similar to embroidery couching and is worked as follows: Thread the end of the no. 2 cane down through the hole next to the corner at the back of the right hand rail and up again in the corner hole with a short end of about 50 mm (2 in.). Lay this end down over the holes in the side rail and after thinning the end of one of your short pieces of no. 6 cane, push it into the corner hole to lie over the short end of no. 2 cane and peg it with a temporary peg. With the long end of the no. 2 cane go down through the same hole as you came up, but over the beading cane, thereby holding it firmly in position over the pegged hole. Pass the long end along underneath the seat to the next open hole and go up and over the beading cane and down again as before. Continue in this way until you reach the front corner, when your couching cane will be in the last hole before the corner. When that hole has been couched take the cane across the corner underneath the seat, to come up in the first hole in the front rail. Thin down this end of the no. 6 cane and put it into the corner hole, and after thinning another piece to go along the front rail, put it in the corner hole at right angles to the first piece. Before laying it down over the holes, peg the corner hole with a permanent peg, and then lay the new piece down along the front rail. In this way your corner peg is covered (see diagrams 7 and 8). Continue couching across the front rail and complete the corner as before. Work the left hand rail in the same manner and then the back rail. When you have completed the back rail and reached your starting point remove the temporary peg and thread the couching cane up in the corner and then back under the last couching. Put the thinned end of the last piece of no. 6 cane into the corner hole and peg it firmly. This is the only peg that will show if you have done it correctly. (See photograph 1.)

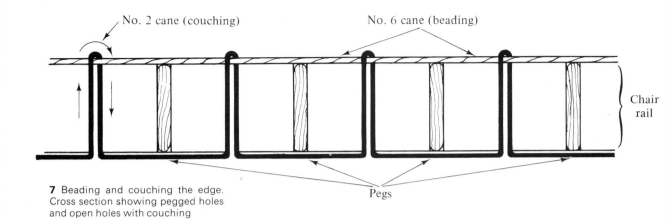

7 Beading and couching the edge. Cross section showing pegged holes and open holes with couching

No. 2 cane (couching)

No. 6 cane (beading)

Chair rail

Pegs

8 Beading and couching

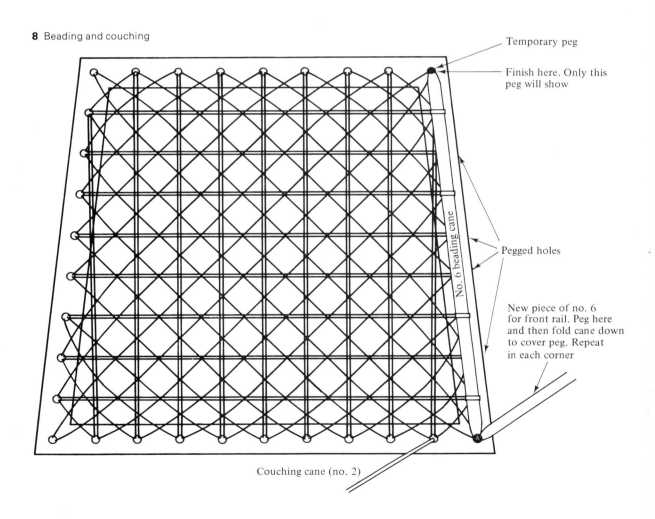

Temporary peg

Finish here. Only this peg will show

No. 6 beading cane

Pegged holes

New piece of no. 6 for front rail. Peg here and then fold cane down to cover peg. Repeat in each corner

Couching cane (no. 2)

If when doing the couching and beading you have difficulty in getting the couching cane through the hole because so many canes are already in it, open the hole gently with the stiletto. Be careful not to push the stiletto through the canes to split them, but put it in against the wood of the frame, and you will find that the cane will go in easily.

The directions I have given so far have been for straight sided or rectangular seats and chairs, but there are a great many which have rounded corners and sometimes shaped rails and backs. This can create problems, and as there is so much variation in the shapes it is almost impossible to give precise instructions—each one must be worked to its own design. The first four stages are usually straightforward, and with the diagonals the great guideline is to keep the rhythm of the pattern working—over verticals and under horizontals and vice versa as the case may be. Wherever you have curves you must adapt the diagonals to them, but always keeping them true to their name as far as possible. (See photograph 4.)

If you study the diagram of the seat with rounded corners (diagram 9), you will see that on the curve you will have to put more than one pair of canes into the holes—at least two and perhaps three pairs will be necessary. When using the 6 way pattern on a seat or back that is curved there are two ways of achieving a good result.

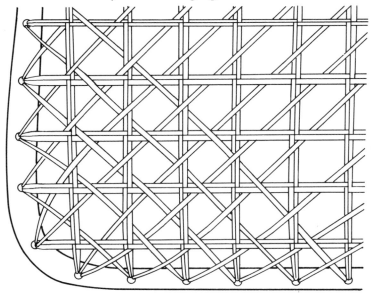

9 Detail of chair seat with rounded corners

3 Bedroom chair, showing how the diagonal pattern is adapted on the two sides, by putting two strands into one hole, or missing holes as necessary

The first one is to work stage one as usual on the curved rails, and when you are ready to do stage two, instead of putting it on top of stage one as is usual, pass the cane underneath stage one so that it takes on the curve. Do not pull the cane too tightly, but let it lie easily under the curve and allow a little play for the later weaves. Then do stage three again underneath stage one and two, and again do not pull tight. When this is complete, stage four can be worked, weaving across as in the original pattern, followed by the two diagonals in the usual way. None of these weaves should be worked tightly, as it is very easy to distort the curve, which spoils the look of the finished seat, and as long as the tension is firm it will be satisfactory.

The second way of working on a curved frame is to work two canes side by side in each hole on the curved rails, again not too tightly. These really represent stages one and three being worked at the same time. Then start to weave over one and under one from side to side, being careful to keep the curve, and again putting two strands into each hole and weaving them alternately to make your darning weave. (See diagram 10.) When this is complete, the two diagonal stages can be worked as before, again being careful to avoid distortion. Both these methods work out well, and I do not think there is much difference in the amount of time they take.

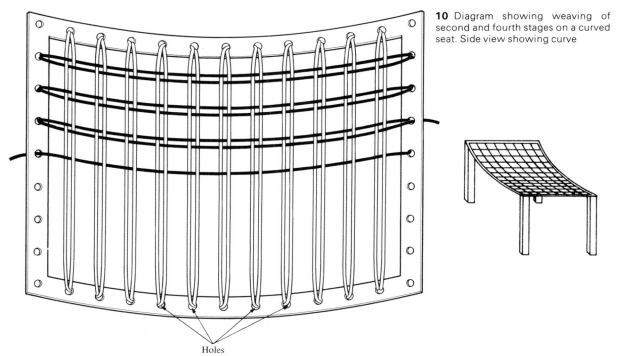

10 Diagram showing weaving of second and fourth stages on a curved seat. Side view showing curve

Holes

4 A Bentwood chair of unusual shape, made in Austria, which clearly shows the method of working diagonals on rounded corners

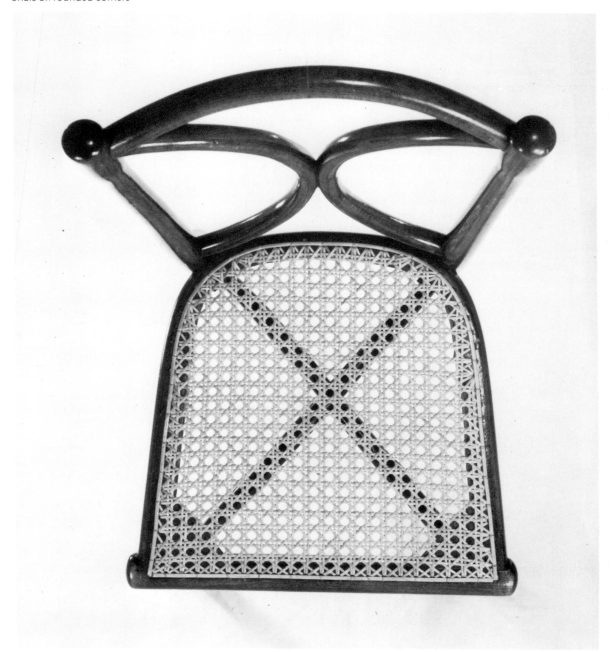

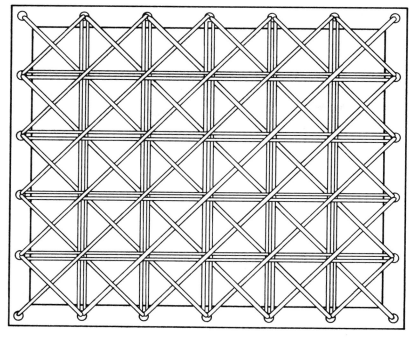

Another 6 way pattern which is very attractive is what we may call 'quick' pattern—meaning that it can be worked very quickly, but I must warn you that it is not as strong or as hardwearing as the design already described. It makes a good ornamental seat, but not one that is wanted for wear. (See diagram 11.)

Materials

No. 3 cane for stages one and two.

No. 4 cane for stages three and four.

This seat is worked with no. 3 and no. 4 cane. Starting with no. 3, stage one is worked by taking two strands of cane from the holes in the back rail to the front (two strands in each hole). These are laid as far as possible side by side. Stage two repeats this by taking two strands in the same manner from side to side. Stage three is a diagonal taken from the right hand back corner to the front left hand corner and it is just laid on top of the four canes already in position, and continued right across the seat from each hole. This is worked with no. 4 cane. The final stage is also worked with no. 4 cane, and is the only stage that is woven. Starting at the back left hand corner peg the cane into the corner hole and then take it over the first diagonal and then under the cross formed by the first two stages, then over the next diagonal and under the next cross, and in this manner right across the seat. Repeat this movement in each hole until the seat is complete. (See photograph 5.)

I should mention that this pattern is only suitable on a square or rectangular seat—I do not think the diagonals would work out correctly on a shaped one.

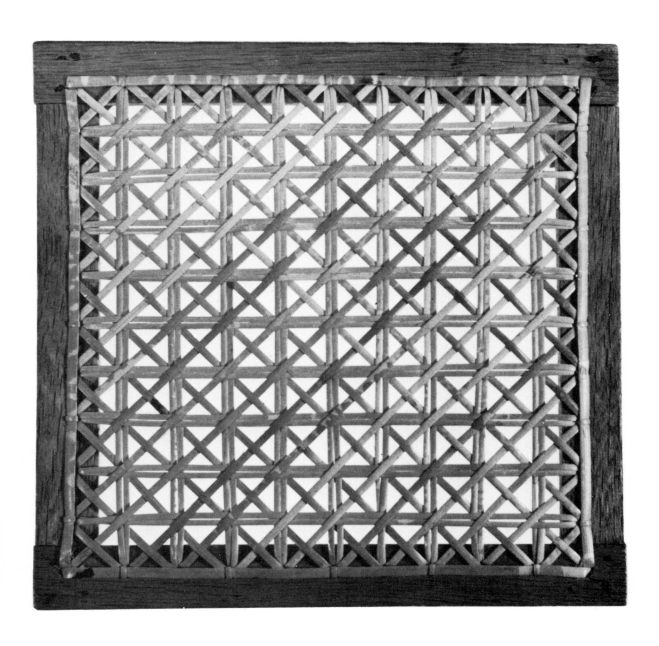

5 6 way pattern seat using the quick method—only one diagonal is actually woven

CANE SEATING 4 WAY PATTERN

Materials
No. 4 cane for stages one and two
No. 3 cane for stages three and four

First method

There are three ways of seating a stool or chair in the 4 way pattern, and the materials and tools used for all of them are the same as described in the 6 way pattern, and the preparation is also the same. In the 4 way pattern, however, a wider cane (no. 4) is used for the first two stages and the narrower one (no. 3) for the diagonals—this is in order to give added strength. None of the 4 way patterns is as strong as the 6 way, but they make very attractive seats, especially on a chair or stool which does not get really hard wear, such as a bedroom chair.

Stage one
This stage is commenced in exactly the same way as the 6 way pattern, but using no. 4 cane. Start in the centre as before and work out to the sides. If you are working on a square or rectangular seat do not use the corner holes until you start the diagonal weaves, but on a shaped seat you may have to use the two corner holes in the back rail—it depends on the spacing of the holes. Adjust the extra holes at the front as shown. (See diagrams 12 and 13.)

Stage two
Still using no. 4 cane weave across the seat from side to side, interweaving each row over and under the canes of the first stage.

Stage three diagram 14
This is the first diagonal, and is worked with no. 3 cane, peg the cane into the right hand corner of the back rail and carefully lay it across from that corner to the appropriate hole in the front or left side rail. The cane should lie on top of the previous two stages diagonally over each crossing of stage one and two. On a square or rectangular seat you will not have to miss any holes, but if you are working a shaped seat, you must adjust the pattern on the side rails as given in the 6 way pattern, and using every hole except the corners, in the back and front rails. (See diagrams 15 and 16.)

Stage four
This is the second diagonal, and is worked from the left hand corner in the back rail across to the right hand side, but this one is woven. It will come from the back corner hole and over the first diagonal, then

under the crossing of the three previous stages, over the next diagonal, and under the crossings again. Continue in this way until you reach the right hand front or side rail, and then continue working backwards and forwards across the seat to complete the pattern.

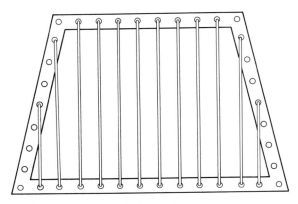

12 4 way pattern, first stage, *not* using corner holes

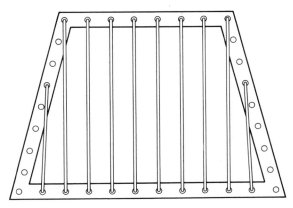

13 4 way pattern, first stage, using corner holes

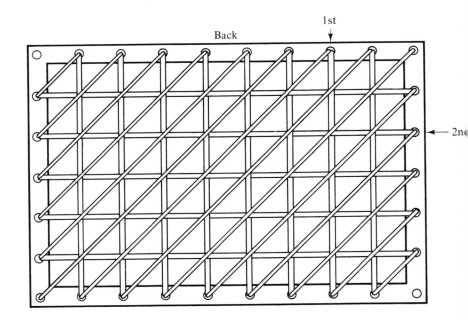

14 4 way pattern, first diagonal

Back

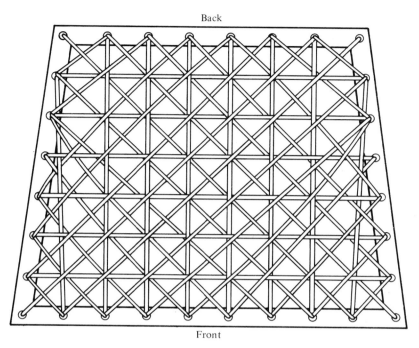

Front

15 4 way pattern, shaped seat, first method

Back

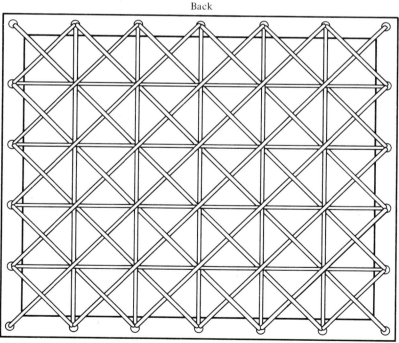

Front

16 rectangular 4 way pattern, first method: first stage back to front; second stage side to side interwoven; third stage (first diagonal) laid on top; fourth stage (second diagonal) interwoven

Second method (see diagram 17)

Stage one

This is worked in exactly the same way as in the first method, still using no. 4 cane.

Stage two

Stage two is worked from side to side, but on top of stage one and not interwoven as before.

Stage three

Now using no. 3 cane peg a length into the back right hand corner, and weave it over the first horizontal and to the left under the first vertical cane. Then take it forward over the next horizontal cane and then left under the next vertical cane. Continue like this until you reach the front left hand corner or the side rail. It does not matter where the cane comes out—it all depends on the shape of the seat—but try and keep a true diagonal line. Work right across the seat in this way until all the holes in the back and front rails are worked, excepting the corners. In this pattern you will find that you can put two canes into the corners, as shown in the 6 way pattern, and this is a good thing to do for extra strength. (See photograph 6.)

NOTE You cannot do this in the first method—your corners can only have one cane in.

17 4 way pattern, second method: first stage back to front; second stage side to side (laid on top); third stage (first diagonal) woven *under* uprights and *over* vertical from right to left canes; fourth stage (second diagonal) woven from left to right *under* vertical and *over* upright canes

Back

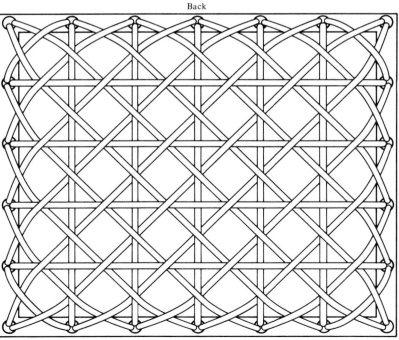

Front

Stage four

This diagonal reverses the weaving of the previous stage. You will now start in the back left hand corner and take the cane forward under the first horizontal and to the right over the first vertical cane, then forward under the next horizontal cane and over the next vertical cane, continuing in this way until the stage is complete.

6 4-way pattern worked by the second method (shaped seat)

Third method

This is a very quick method, but I must emphasise that it has not the strength and good wearing qualities of the previous patterns. The first three stages are all laid on top of each other with no weaving at all—the first is from back to front, the second is from side to side, and the third is diagonally across from the back right corner to the front or side rail on the left hand side. The fourth stage is the only one to be woven, and will be worked from the back left hand corner, going under the crossings and over the first diagonal all the way across the seat. (See photograph 6.)

This pattern is not very practical on a shaped seat. All these different methods may be finished either by pegging each hole and then cutting off all the ends underneath, or by beading and couching the edge as shown in the 6 way pattern.

SHAPED CANE BACKS

Materials
No. 2 cane for first four stages
No. 3 cane for last two stages
No. 6 and no. 2 cane for beading and couching if required

7 4 way pattern worked by the first method (shaped seat)

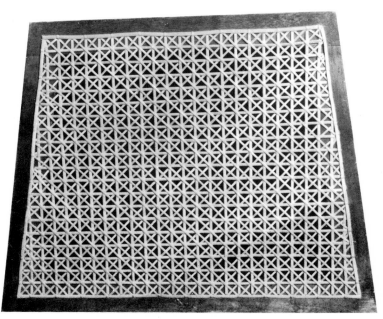

8 A handsome chair with oval seat and circular back, all worked in 6 way pattern

9 A chair of Jacobean style with oval back worked in 6 way pattern

There are many fancy patterns woven on the backs of chairs which are sometimes cane-seated and sometimes upholstered. Some of these ornamental backs have either a round or an oval wooden medallion in the centre, and when caned give a sun ray effect. I have included pictures showing some of these which are usually worked in the 6 way pattern. If you have one which is in need of re-caning, it is a great help if you sketch out a chart of perhaps a half-section of the design. Mark the number of holes in the medallion and also the number in the outer frame and trace where each cane from the medallion goes out to the frame. (See photograph 10.)

Where the canes are splaying out from a small circular centre to a larger rectangular frame you will find that the first four stages are fairly straightforward, but the diagonals are more difficult, as they will be curving into their holes. Careful study of the chart will show you how this works. If you cut out the old seat without charting it first, you will find it very confusing to sort out where each cane should go.

The first and third stages of the 6 way pattern are worked first from the medallion to the frame. First of all, tie the medallion in its place with fine string or thread at the four points of the compass, making certain that it is absolutely central. Then cut lengths of no. 2 cane, long enough to reach from the frame to the medallion and back again. Peg in the end of the cane on the frame and take it over and thread it into the medallion, out through the next hole and back again to the frame. If this is done all round the medallion with the first and third movements, you will then have two canes in each hole, radiating out from the medallion. Try to ensure that the third movement fills in the gaps left by the first stage on the back of the medallion, so that there is a continuous line of cane round it. This is not important from the point of view of the caning, but it does give a more professional finish to the work. All the ends of the canes will be in the holes on the outer frame of the chair. You will probably find that you have a few more holes in the frame than in the medallion, and therefore must miss some—try to do this on the lower sides of the frame.

The second and fourth stages are worked in a circle round the medallion, being woven over and under each cane of the first and third stages, with the end of each circle overlapping its beginning by about 50 mm (2 in.). The weaving should be alternate on each row. About 7 circles are generally necessary, each consisting of two rows of cane with about 13 mm ($\frac{1}{2}$ in.) intervals between each pair. The circles

10 Chair with caned arms and back worked in 'sun ray' pattern

will get a little wider apart as you get out towards the frame of the chair. The corners will need to be filled in on the outer frame with one or two short rows. (See photographs 8, 9 and 10.) When putting in the diagonals, using no. 3 cane peg the end into the medallion and work outwards, following the routine of over and under each pair of canes in the usual way, and ensuring that the diagonals are running in the little grooves formed in the first four stages, as emphasised in the first pattern. If you follow this routine correctly, you will find that the diagonals will curve round towards the outer frame. When both the diagonal stages are completed, peg all the holes very firmly, using tiny pegs for the medallion and large ones for the frame, and make sure that none of these pegs are protruding through the back of the chair. If you can arrange your weaving so that the cane covers every gap between the holes on the back of the frame, it will add a good finish to the work. (See diagram 18 and photograph 11.)

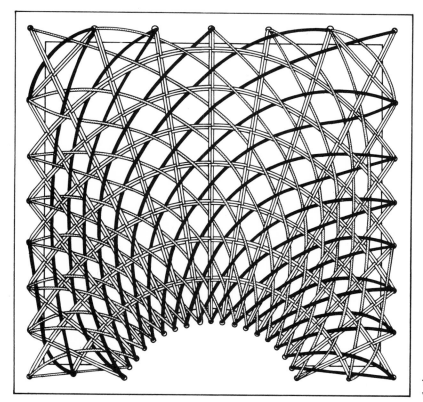

18 Chair with 'Rising Sun' back (6 way pattern)

There are also circular seats and oval seats woven with cane, and all these varying designs do pose some problems. With circular seats, for instance, where you have no corners to use as a guide to the correct working of the diagonals, it is a good plan to mark four holes in the frame at suitable places, to represent the corners, and use them as you used the corners in the first pattern, by putting two canes in the one hole. The only difference will be that instead of only having one corner hole with two diagonal canes in it, you will probably have to put two canes into three or perhaps four of the holes round the curves where you have marked the holes. This will keep the diagonals at their true angle. (See diagram 19.) If you wish to bead and couch the edge of a circular seat, it would be wise to damp the no. 6 cane well before using it, so that it can be shaped round the curves to lie flat.

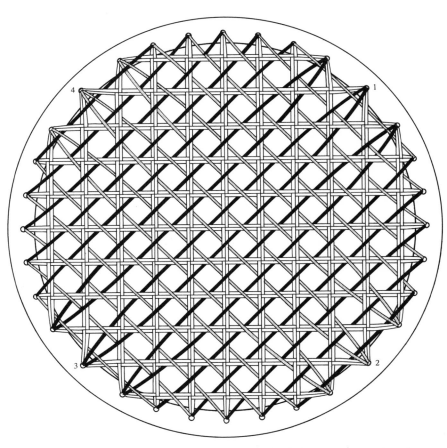

19 Circular chair seat, showing arrangement of diagonals

There is another 6 way pattern seat, which is very attractive, but also very complicated. See photographs 12 and 13.

Materials
No. 2 cane for stage one
No. 4 cane for stages two, three and four
No. 3 cane for stages five and six
The weaving begins with no. 2 cane taken from back to front of the seat, taken in every hole. The second stage consists of a side to side movement, with no. 4 cane in every alternate hole. The next two stages are also woven with no. 4 cane in what I must call 'upright' diagonals, the first woven from right to left, and the second from left to right. As the horizontal canes are two spaces apart, the angle of the diagonal is altered. Pegging your piece of cane in the back right hand

corner, weave it over the horizontal canes and under the vertical ones, and again using alternate holes. You will probably have to do some adjusting on the side rails to keep the lines as straight as possible. When this stage is completed, peg your next piece of no. 4 cane into the left back corner and weave again over the horizontal canes and under the vertical ones, but passing under the diagonal you have just completed and again using alternate holes. Both these diagonals should start and finish in the same holes. (See detail.) The last two stages are also diagonals, but 'long' ones, as you will see in the detail—the one from right to left is woven over the first horizontal, under the first upright and second diagonal where they cross each other, over the second upright, under the next upright and diagonal, and over the horizontal and first diagonal where they cross, and under the upright and diagonal again. Continue this weave right across the seat from alternate holes on the back and front rails, but *not* the holes used for the previous two diagonal stages. These last two stages are woven with no. 3 cane. The final stage starts from the left hand corner and is worked under the first and third diagonals, over the first upright then under the first and third diagonals together with the next upright, over the second diagonal and the horizontal where they cross, and under the first and third diagonal and the next upright, over the next upright and third diagonal, and then under the first and third diagonals and the next upright again, repeating this sequence right across the seat. Here again you will use the alternate holes on the back and front rails, using the holes which carry the one upright cane and the third diagonal cane. You will find that a little adapting of the pattern is needed on the side rails.

There is one snag that you may possibly meet when doing the cane seating, and that is having 'blind holes'. These are holes which do not go right through the frame, and therefore you cannot thread the cane through. If you look at the back of the frame, you may see that there is a narrow piece of wood inserted in a groove. This means that the holes are in the groove, and the wood has been put in to cover the holes after the seating was done. You must remove this little spline of wood (a carpenters job, usually) and when the seating is completed, put it back again. If the holes are not covered in this way, but are completely blind, as they sometimes are when they go through into a leg of the chair, you will have to cut each cane short and put it into the hole with a temporary peg, until all the stages are complete, and then peg permanently.

12 Stool seated in hexagonal pattern

11 Chair with caned back in fan shaped pattern. 6 way

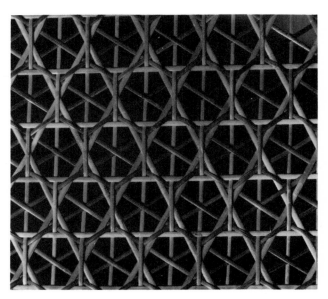

13 Detail of hexagonal pattern

CLOSE CANING

This caning is worked much more easily on a square or rectangular seat, than on a shaped one, and it is advisable to have plenty of practical experience before attempting it on a chair.

First of all the seat must have a 'liner' inside the frame, which can be made from fairly thick centre cane (no. 10 or no. 12) or palembang brown cane. This is attached inside the frame by panel pins, or can be tied on each rail with fine string, which can be removed as the work proceeds. (See diagram 20.) Measure the centre cane along the rail, and bend it with round-nosed pliers to fit as closely as possible into the corner of each rail. Cut the ends with a long diagonal cut, so that they fit together neatly where they join. (See diagram 20.)

You will also need a 'tension rod' which is a small rod or stick over which the warp is put on to the seat thus allowing 'play' for the weaving you will do afterwards. No precise instructions can be given as to the thickness of this rod, it really depends on whether you weave tightly or loosely. The rod I use is 15 mm ($\frac{5}{8}$ in.) wide and about 6 mm ($\frac{1}{4}$ in.) in thickness, and I am a medium worker. The rod must be long enough to lie across the seat and rest on top of the two side rails.

If your stool is a fairly large one—anything over about 30 cm (12 in.) square—you need to put in some 'base caning' before you start the actual seat. You will probably find that there are a few holes in each of the four rails, usually about 38–50 mm ($1\frac{1}{2}$–2 in.) apart, and these should be caned first to form a strong support for the seat. Use a wider cane (no. 4 or 5 would be suitable) and thread the cane from the back rail to the front, putting two strands in each hole. Then interweave on these from one side to the other, again putting two canes in each hole and then peg each hole firmly, taking care that the pegs are flush with the surface of the rail.

This base caning is not done on a small stool. (See diagram 21.) You are now ready to start on the actual seat. Prepare your cane by damping as usual, and use no. 3 if it is a small stool or no. 4 for a larger one. Put the tension rod across the stool at about the centre of the frame, and then cut the cane into lengths long enough to go from front to back and over and under both rails, with about 76 mm (3 in.) to spare at each end. Mark the centre of the front and back rail, and commencing at the front bring the cane over the mark on the front rail and underneath the rail, then bring the end up in the centre of the seat, over the cane itself and the liner and thread it down between the liner and the frame. Take the other end of the cane over your tension stick and repeat this knotting on the back rail. (See diagram 22.)

20 Close caning. 'Liner' tied in position inside frame. Gaps have been left to show how it is placed – it would of course fit closely into the frame. Tie with strong thread; the ties can be removed as you work

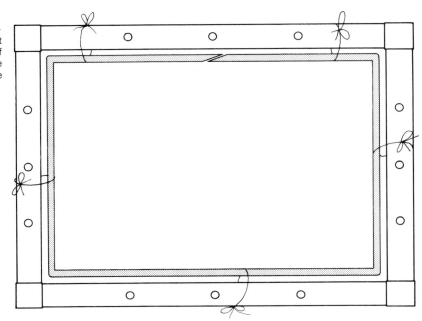

21 Base for close caning with liner in place, the threads holding it in each corner

Join in cane liner

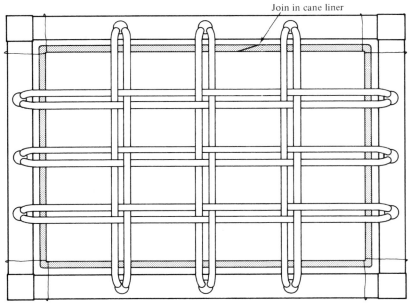

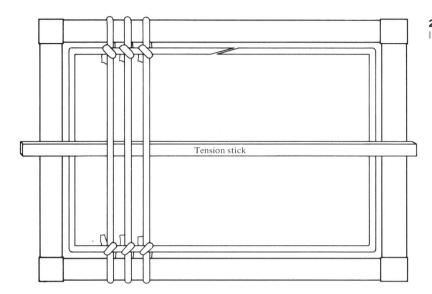

Tension stick

Continue working in the same way until you have completed one side of the seat, making sure that all the knots are going in the same direction, and pushing each strand very closely up to the next one. You will find this easier to do when you have completed about 50 mm (2 in.) of the weaving. Starting again in the centre, work out to the other side in the same manner until the warp is complete. Make sure that the strands of cane are very close together, and the rail is completely covered. You may find that you will have to wrap the cane once or twice round the rail in the corners as the width of the liner prevents another strand being put in.

Commence weaving on this warp—starting on the right hand side, and again measuring the cane lengths as you did for the warp. Knot the cane on the right hand rail and then thread it over three warp strands and then under three all the way across the seat and knot again on the left hand rail. If the tension rod is in your way push it towards the back of the seat, and it can be removed altogether when about a quarter of the seat is woven. Starting again on the right hand side, thread the cane under one strand then ★ over three and under three, repeating from ★ to the end of the row. The third row will commence under two strands and then over three and under three to the end. If you continue in this way, threading the weaving cane one strand further to the left on each row, you will achieve a very pleasing diagonal pattern. (See diagram 23.) This pattern can also be varied if you mark the half-way stage on each side rail, and when you reach the mark reverse the weaving, making it into an arrowhead design.

Try not to catch the base caning underneath the seat in your weaving—it is sometimes a little difficult to avoid, but you will have a neater finish if you can do so.

It is a good idea to have a damp cloth or sponge beside you while you are working, so that you can keep the cane damped. It is apt to dry out very quickly from the warmth of your hands.

When you are within two or three rows of completing the weaving, if you find that you have misjudged the thickness of the

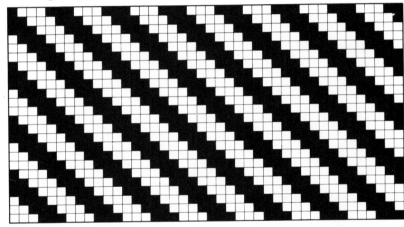

23 Design given in text on close caning

24 Design for close cane or cord seat

tension rod, and the weaving is either too tight or too loose, carefully sponge the canes on the back rail with a wet sponge, and when they are damp loosen each knot and re-knot it at the correct tension. When finished leave the cane to dry out completely, and then all the ends underneath the seat can be cut off very closely.

There are a great many designs that can be used for these seats, some of which are shown here and almost any block or counted thread design could be adapted. (See diagrams 22, 23, 24 and 25.)

Some people find it easier to weave on the warp with a long wire needle, and these are easy to obtain. I always prefer to work with my fingers.

25 Design for close cane or cord seat

14 Chair seated in close caning

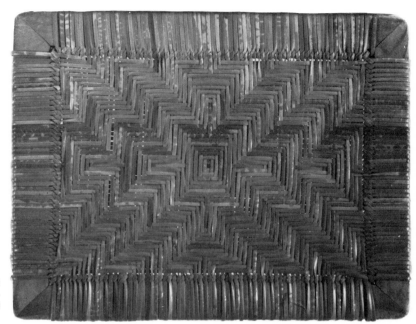

15, 16, 17 Various designs for close caning or cord seats. Any good counted thread design can be used for this type of seat

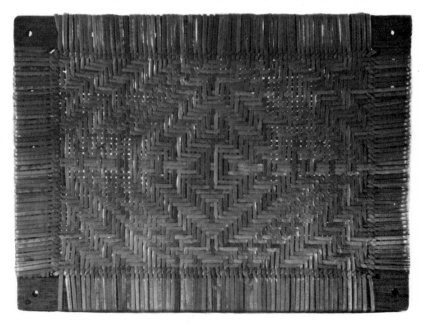

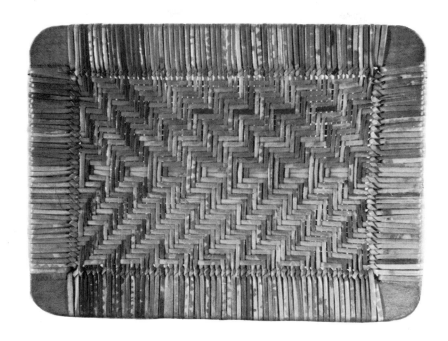

26 Design for close cane or cord seat

Rush seating

The craft of rushwork has a very special appeal to any worker in natural materials, as rushes are so much a part of the English countryside. I think it is true to say that most basic crafts—pottery, weaving, basketry—have grown up from primitive beginnings where people tried to use any materials that came to hand to make for themselves aids to improve their comfort and their usefulness to the community. In early times, rushes and sedge were widely used to cover the rough floors of the rooms in which the family or community lived, and these rushes would be left on the floor from one year to the next when the new harvest would bring a fresh supply. Rushes were still being strewn on the floors in early Tudor times, and I think it is not fanciful to suggest that during the short dark days of winter, someone would probably start to twist and plait the rushes together to make a neater and more manageable floor covering. In this way would slowly have evolved the beautiful rush basketry and seating which is found everywhere today, and which affords such great pleasure to its owners.

The colouring and texture of rush has the advantage of looking right with any period of furniture and furnishing. It is equally at home with antique furniture or ultra modern.

The rushes we use are the home-grown variety—the English green rushes or *Scirpus Lacustris* to give them their Latin name. These are the true bulrushes. The tall plant growing in the dykes and marshy places, with a brown velvety top, which as children we knew as bulrushes, are not rushes at all, but reeds, and that particular one is the Great Reed Mace. The true bulrush has only a small panicle of tiny brown flowerets right at the top of the stem and can be identified by this. There is also a small rush which is much shorter and softer—*Juncus Effusis*—which can be used to make attractive small articles, but is not suitable for seating.

The seating of chairs and stools with rushes is a most rewarding occupation on account of the pleasure of using this delightfully soft and adaptable material, and also because a really worthwhile result can be attained with care and patience. Their colouring has great variety, ranging from dark green through the lighter shades to beautiful orange, yellow and brownish colours. They grow from about 1·8–3 m (6–10 ft) high and are found in rivers, ponds and marshy areas.

Rushes for seating are also imported from abroad, notably from Holland—these are very strong and hardwearing though not quite as long as the English ones, and mostly in golden and fawn shades, possibly due to the fact that they are salt water rushes. All the rushes are beautifully soft and silky to handle when properly prepared and are a real joy to use. The ones I generally use come from Huntingdon, as I find it advisable to buy them direct from the growers, so that they come in the best possible condition. They are sold by the 'bolt' which is a large bundle about 3 m (10 ft) tall, and measuring about 100 cm (40 in.) round the base. As the rushes taper from the base to the top, the bundle is conical in shape. They need to be stored in a cool and airy place, and can stand upright against a wall or in a corner. A good way of storing them is to sling some netting from one side of a shed or garage to the other as a hammock and lay them in this. In this way they will get the air all round them. Do not put them anywhere that is at all damp or they will get mould on them, and lose their colouring. They can be kept for a long time if properly stored—I have used some that were over two years old, and they worked perfectly.

The rushes are usually cut every alternate year, so that they can grow to full maturity. The growers therefore generally have two sets of beds, so that one can be cut each year. The time for harvesting is late July, though this does depend on the weather—if we have a cold wet summer it would probably be later. Although they grow in or near water, they need the sun to mature them, and a cold rainy summer can mean a poor crop. They are cut under water, as far down as possible, and are then spread out in the air to dry, in a shady place. Strong sunlight should be avoided as it takes away some of their delicate colouring, and although they would still retain a variety of shades, they would be somewhat dimmed.

They should not be bent during the drying process, or they will be weakened at the bend. I have seen them drying over a wire fence along the river bank. Care should be taken that they are completely dried before tying them into bundles, so that they do not get mould from inside the bundle. When thoroughly dry they can be tied up into bolts, ready for sale. It must be understood that they *are* a harvest—like corn—and once the grower has sold his stock, there will be no more until the following year.

The bolts contain rushes of many different thicknesses and lengths, and it is a useful idea, when you receive the bolt, to sort the rushes into about three sizes—thick, medium, and thin—judging them from the thick end, which is called the *butt*. The thin end is called the *tip*.

Rush seating does not require many tools. Apart from scissors and a ruler or measure, the only other necessary tools are a steel rush needle, and a wooden padding stick, which can be made easily from the handle of an old wooden spoon with the bowl cut off, and the end shaped and thinned as in diagram 27. A chair or stool for rush seating needs the raised corners to hold the rushes in place. (See photograph 18.) If you are using the rushes for basketry, you will need some of each size, according to the article you intend to make, but for seating you require mostly the fine and medium ones, and it is wise when ordering to specify that you want seating rushes.

The rushes must be dampened before use to make them supple. I usually pick out thirty or forty rushes which are the correct size for my purpose, and damp them in the bath to avoid bending them. Put the butt ends in cold or tepid water and carefully fold round the thinner ends to get the whole length into the water. Put a cloth or sponge on top of them to keep them under the water and leave them for 1 to 2 minutes, then take them out and fold them in half to make a shorter bundle and wrap them tightly in a towel or piece of blanket. They will fold safely when damp, but not when they are dry. It is advisable to prepare them in this way the night before you wish to use them—they will then be at their best in the morning—not wet, but soft and supple. Do not damp more than you think you can use at one time, as although they can be dried off and re-damped, it is better to use them after the first damping.

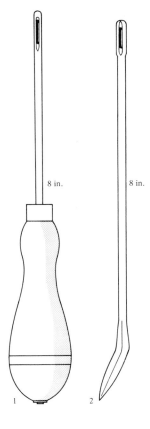

27 Tools for rush seating (also cord)

8 in.   8 in.

1   2

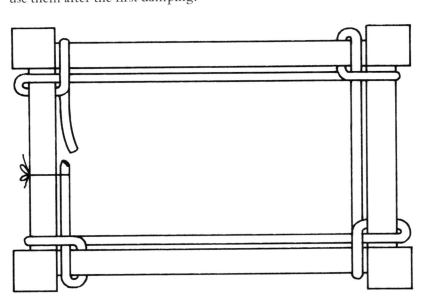

28 Diagram showing how beginning of rush seat is effected: coil away from corner

RUSH SEATING (RECTANGULAR)

My first instruction will be for seating a rectangular stool, and having prepared the rushes as suggested, pick out two similar in size as far as possible—they should be a good medium size—about 19 mm ($\frac{3}{4}$ in.) in width when pressed flat at the butt end. It is usual to use two rushes together, putting the tip of one with the butt of the other and coiling them together to form a coil that is even in thickness. Before using them wipe them with a piece of rag to remove any dirt that may be on them, and also to press out the air. Always wipe from the tip to the butt to avoid splitting the rush when the air is forced out. The tips are generally rather brittle and need to be removed, so test them by holding the rush in your left hand about 254 mm (10 in.) from the top, and with the right hand give a small tug at the tip—if it breaks, repeat the process. Do not be too rough with it—you are not *trying* to break it, only testing to remove the fragile part. Having done this with your two rushes, place them tip to butt and tie them tightly together about 25 mm (1 in.) from the end. Tie with a fine string—a flax string is the most suitable—and take this string round the left hand side rail of the stool, about 15 cm (6 in.) from the corner, tying it tightly so that the rushes and the knot are on the inside of the frame. The rushes are now twisted together to form a smooth coil—hold them just inside the front rail with the left hand, and with the right hand press them together to force out the air and carefully coil them to go over the front rail, and down the front of the rail—the coil is always *away from* the corner, not towards it. (See diagram 28.)

Keep the coil as smooth and even as possible—do not twist one rush round the other, but work both together. (See diagram 29.) The rush should be coiled only on the top of the seat, and down the front of the rail—just the part that will show—all the rushes on the under side of the seat are kept as flat as possible, so that they 'bed' into each other, making a neat finish underneath. Try to keep the underneath as tidy as you can, covering the knots and tucking the ends away.

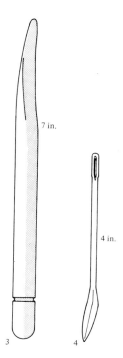

7 in.

4 in.

3   4

Bring the coil back under the front rail and up in the centre of the seat, then to the left over the left hand rail, starting to coil again just before it reaches the rail. Take it down and underneath the left hand rail again, and across the seat, coiling again to go over the right hand rail. (See diagram 28 for sequence of weaving.) Pull the rush fairly tightly across the seat, but at the corners be very careful to keep the two crossings that form the corner absolutely at right angles to each other, so that the corners are not pulled out of shape. (See diagrams 30 and 31.) Where the rushes need joining, use a reef knot where you have come to the end of a rush, or half-hitch if you wish to add an extra rush to one that is too thin. Both these knots are shown in diagrams 32 and 33. Joins may be made anywhere in the middle part of the rails, but not near the corners or they might distort the weaving. If one rush is longer than the other, they can be joined separately, and it is not always necessary to use two rushes

29 Rush coil for seating: A is correct, B is wrong

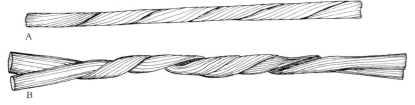

A

B

30 Rush seat, keeping corners at right angles
31 How *not* to make a rush seat

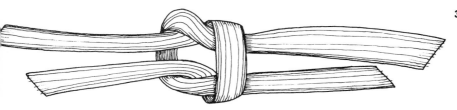

32 Reef knot for rush work

together—it depends on your bundle of rushes. If it consists of a number of thicker rushes, you can use one alone, adding another thin end by means of a half-hitch when the first one begins to get thinner. The great point to remember is to keep the thickness of the coil as even as possible—nothing looks worse than a seat with thick and thin ones lying indiscriminately side by side. If you have a great many thinner rushes, use three or even four together if necessary. On a small stool we would reckon on working six coils to 25 mm (1 in.), or five coils to 25 mm (1 in.) on a slightly larger one.

When you have completed about one third of the seat, do some padding in the corners. The idea of padding is to raise the coils of rush just above the edges of the wooden frame on the inner side, so that the seat will be more hard wearing. The padding is done on the under side, so turn the stool upside down, and you will see that you have eight little pockets—two at each corner of the stool. Any short pieces of rush can be used for padding, or any broken pieces, but make sure that they are absolutely dry—if you use damp pieces they may spoil the look of your seat by turning mouldy. Fold the pieces up into small bunches and push them into each pocket as far as you can, either with your fingers or the padding stick. Do not use too much padding at a time, but build it up slowly—it is only necessary to raise the coils slightly above the rail, and this will tighten your weave and make the seat stronger.

It is not wise to try and complete a seat in one operation. The rushes will shrink a little when they dry out, and you will find that the coils can be closed up after a day or so, and you can therefore get a firmer finish. I usually work a seat in three stages—when about one third is done, I leave it for twenty-four hours and can then push the coils up close together, and continue with another section. Remember to pad underneath after working every few centimetres, and when the coils on the side rails get within 50 mm (2 in.) of each other, pad right across the gap, as otherwise you will have difficulty in getting the padding in.

Having filled up the two side rails with coils as closely packed together as possible, you will find that you have a section in the centre of the seat which should be filled by a figure of eight weave, working over the front rail—underneath and up in the centre space and over the back rail, again underneath and up in the centre and over the front rail again. Continue in this way until the space is completely filled. It is advisable before starting the figure of eight movement to mark the exact centre of the front and back rails, and on reaching the mark when working the figure of eight, reverse the weave—instead of coiling away from the corner, coil towards it, so that although you will actually finish the coils a little to one side of the centre, the coils themselves will meet in the middle of the rail. This makes a neater and more symmetrical finish. (See photograph 18.) When the space is completely filled, finish off by knotting your final strand to the strand opposite to it on the underside, using the rush needle, and then tuck away the end under the weaving.

33 Half-hitch

18 Rush seated stool

RUSH SEATING (SHAPED)

Where you have a shaped chair to be seated with rush, your first problem is to fill in the extra space on the front rail, before you can work in the sequence as shown for the rectangular or square seat. This can be done in three different ways, according to the size and shape of the chair.

First method

The first method is most suitable for the normal sized bedroom or dining chair, where the seat is almost square—perhaps about 50 mm (2 in.) difference in length between the back and front rail. We will suppose that the front rail *is* 50 mm (2 in.) longer than the back one, and assuming that you are working 5 coils to measure 25 mm (1 in.), you will need five pairs of rushes of medium thickness, and every pair will make one coil on each side of the front and side rail, thus filling 25 mm (1 in.) on each side. (See diagram 35.) After testing the tips and wiping down the rushes, put five tips and five butts together and tie them tightly with the flax string into one bunch, and then tie them to the rail on the left hand side of the chair, just inside the rail and about half way between the back and front corners. Take one of these pairs consisting of one butt and one tip and coil them together smoothly, over the front rail—down the front and up in the centre of the seat, then over the left side rail and down again underneath—across to the right side rail and over it, down the side and again up in the centre and forward over the front rail on the right hand side. Tie this pair with a temporary tie to the right side rail, about half way along its length. Work each of your other four pairs of rushes in this way, laying each one close to the previous coil and tying off with the temporary tie on the right side rail. When all the five pairs are in position, measure the space between them on the front rail, and also measure the back rail again, and if these two measurements are equal, you can now go round the seat in the same manner as given for the rectangular seat. Before doing this, however, gather up the four pairs which were first worked and tied in the temporary tie, and making sure that the coils are firmly placed on the front rail, tie the loose rushes tightly together with the flax string, and then tie inside the right side rail in the same manner as they were tied on the left rail at the beginning. You can now continue round the seat with the fifth pair in the usual way, joining as and when necessary, as shown in the previous instruction.

There is another join which is very useful where you have a seat with fairly large corners—it is called a *corner join*, and is used when you have completed the first half of the corner and then find that your rushes are too thin to complete the second half satisfactorily. When you bring the two rushes up from underneath to coil them for the second half of the corner, add another thin end of a new rush to them, leaving about 50 mm (2 in.) of its tip underneath the seat, and coil the three rushes together. The coiling will hold the new rush in place, and the end underneath can be tucked away after you have worked another round. This is a very helpful join as you get nearer to the centre of the seat.

Second method

The second method of filling in the extra space on the front rail is by starting with one pair of rushes, tied to the left side rail, and working them all round the seat in the sequence as shown, and when the back left hand corner is completed, separate your two rushes and join another rush to each of them, either with a reef knot or a half-hitch. (See diagram 36.) You can then make two coils with them over the two front corners, combining them again into one coil when you have completed the front right hand corner. This is easy to do with care—if your coil is likely to be too thick when the two coils are put together, try to discard the thicker rushes by tying them to some new thinner ones and keeping the coil as far as possible to an even thickness.

When the whole round is completed, you will have three coils each side of the front corners and only two at the back corners, and you can continue increasing the number of coils at the front by working every alternate row in the same manner. When the space between the coils on the front rail and on the back rail are equal, you can then continue as for the rectangular seat.

This method is very suitable for a chair seat with a difference of more than 76 mm (3 in.) between the measurement of the front and back rail, but it does take a great deal of careful working out.

Third method

The third method consists of working twice round each front corner, and only once round the back corners, on every alternate row until the space is again equal. This is a very good method, but needs great care as the tendency is to pull the corners out of shape when working round them twice, and thus distorting the weaving.

All these methods are completed by padding underneath and finishing off as given for the rectangular seat. Again it is important to keep a smooth and even coil, and to keep a true right angle every time your coil completes a corner.

When it is necessary to discard rushes during weaving, always make quite sure that the discarded rushes are firmly tied off to another rush either by a half-hitch or to a conveniently placed knot. If you leave them just tucked in they may spoil the seat by working loose with wear. I think it advisable also to work any of these seats in the three stages as suggested in the square and rectangular pattern—it will enable you to close the coils more tightly.

Also, try to make the underside of the seats as neat as you can—try to cover the knots wherever possible and 'bed in' each pair of rushes as they are worked. As you get towards the centre this becomes more difficult, but it is well worth the trouble, to get a really good result. When the centre is reached, the bedding in becomes very important, as if it is not done you will have a large lump in the centre, underneath which is very unsightly to look at.

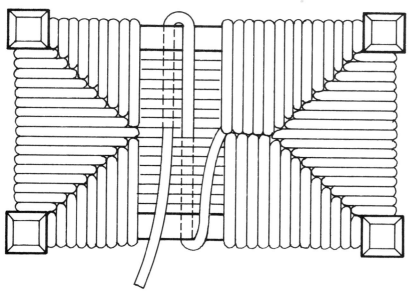

34 Finishing rush stool seat

35 Rush seating: first method of filling in the 'gusset' with rushes on a shaped chair

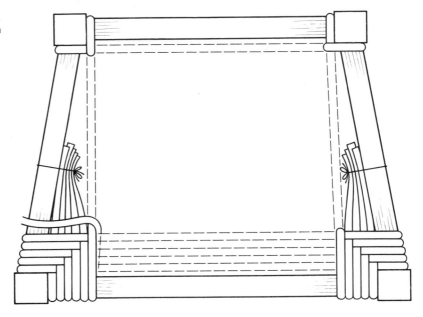

36 Rush seating: second method of filling in the 'gusset' on a shaped chair. When coming from the back left hand corner to the front rail, divide the coil into two parts and join a new rush to each part either with a reef knot or a half-hitch—thus making two coils on the front rail to one at the back. After working the two front corners, combine the two coils into one again for the right hand back rail. Do this on every alternate round

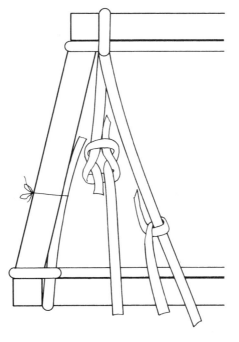

19 Rush 'drop in' chair seat

RUSH SEATING (SCANDINAVIAN)

Shaped seat

The Scandinavian method of rush seating varies slightly from our own—it makes a most attractive seat, and I think it may be helpful to include examples in this book. Choose two rushes of medium thickness to commence the coil and tie them tightly together, and then on the front rail as near to the left corner as possible. Now take them across the seat, starting to coil them just before reaching the right side rail. Go over this and underneath and up in the centre, and then back to the left side rail. Go over this, then underneath and up again over the right side rail. Continue in this way, working to and fro until you have four coils on the right side rail—then bring the coil up in the centre again and forward over the four coils and the front rail, again under and up in the centre, and make one short wrap over the right side rail. Then cross to the left side and over the rail—thus making the fourth coil there—bring the rushes up in the centre, forward over the four coils and the front rail, again up in the centre and a short wrap over the left side rail. Repeat this whole process again three times, and then reduce the number of crossings to three, and then to two. When the distance between the two sets of coils on each side measures the same as the width across the back rail, the ordinary pattern as used for the rectangular seat is worked. The seat is padded and finished as in previous patterns. (See photograph 20.)

The rectangular stool seat in which the corners are also covered with rush coils is another interesting design. The corners will cover most satisfactorily if they are slightly rounded (see photograph 21), and all four corners are completed first, with the coil worked in a figure of eight movement. The main part of the stool is then worked as described in the first rush pattern for the rectangular stool. The coil for this kind of seat looks more suitable if it is slightly thicker than for the previous seats—about four coils to 25 mm (1 in.). The preparation of the rushes is exactly the same as previously given, and also the same attention to the neatness of the underside, and the finishing.

There is an unusual variation in the rush seating which comes from Normandy, in France. These chairs are seated in the rush pattern, but the material is quite different. Instead of rush, a fine sedge is used, and as the stems are very fine about eight or ten strands must be used to make a good coil. When this coil is made it is overwrapped with corn straw of a beautiful golden colour. The overwrapping is only worked on the top of the seat and the depth of the rail—where the coil goes underneath the seat the straw is not used. This makes a very attractive and interesting seat. Of course, it entails a great deal of care in joining in the sedge to keep the continuity and evenness of the coil. (See photograph 22.)

I have seen several chairs seated in this way, and some of them have been overwrapped with straw of two different colours—two coils are worked with a pale straw, and the next two with a darker shade, giving a slightly striped effect over the whole seat. (See photograph 23.)

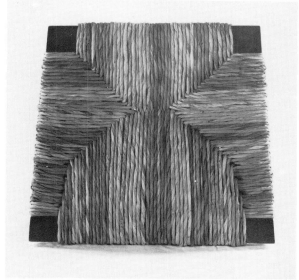

20 Rush seat in Scandinavian style, showing variety of shades in rushes

21 Scandinavian stool seat

22 Chair seat from Normandy, seated with sedge overwrapped with bright gold corn. This is a traditional method of seating in the area

23 Another chair from Normandy, this time overwrapped with two different shades of corn, giving a striped effect

Seating with willows

The use of willow for chair seats was much more widespread in earlier times than it is now—probably because when communications were more difficult than nowadays, and other materials were difficult to find—willows were easily obtained and therefore were made use of. I have seen a willow seat very occasionally in country areas, sometimes in a private house and sometimes in the village inn. They are more likely to be found in the areas where willows are grown in quantity, notably Somerset, East Anglia and Lincolnshire.

There are many different varieties of willow, several of which are suitable for basketry and seating purposes. They grow to their best generally near to water—along the riverside or in low-lying fields adjacent to water. They may be cut either in the spring, when the sap is beginning to flow, or in the late autumn when it is dying down. They consist of long, slender stems of one years' growth, and therefore are without side shoots. The attractive reddish brown colour, which is so popular, is achieved by boiling the willows for several hours, then the colour in the bark will be absorbed into the stems.

This process is known as *buffing the willows*. After the boiling the bark can be removed very easily, leaving the stems buff or brown willows. They can be stripped of their bark without being boiled and will then be white willows, and the two colours used together are very effective.

Actually, when you buy them from the growers they are usually buffed, unless you ask for white ones, but I have cut and buffed them myself. Willows are usually graded and sold by length—92 cm, 106 cm or 120 cm (3 ft, 3 ft 6 in. or 4 ft).

They need to be soaked before use—put them in tepid or cold water for about one to one and a half hours for the small ones—and cover them with a cloth or sponge to keep them down in the water. Take them out at the end of the time, and wrap them tightly in a towel or blanket to 'mellow'. If you can do this overnight, they will be in the best condition for working in the morning. The longer ones, being thicker, will need more soaking to make them supple.

Always remove the tips from the willows before you use them—the tips are always rather brittle. The back rail of the chair is wrapped first along its full length. If you are using the small willows, use them as they are, after removing the tips, but if using the longer willows, split them down into two pieces with a penknife, or into three pieces using a cleave. (See diagram 38.) After being split just scrape the back of each piece with a penknife to remove the pith. A willow 'shave' can be bought for this purpose, but unless you are likely to use it a great deal, it is hardly worth the expense.

As you bind along the back rail, bind in the end of each new willow every time you need to join. At the end of the rail tuck the end of the binding willow under the wrappings. Then commence wrapping the front rail, and when you have completed about one inch bind in the thin end of a new long willow inside the rail, and bring it underneath and over the front rail towards the back. (See diagram 39.) Continue binding, and repeat adding in the new willows at about 38 mm ($1\frac{1}{2}$ in.) intervals across the front rail, spacing the new long willows as evenly as possible, with the wrapping closely between them. All these new long willows must be long enough to be bound in at the front, come up over the rail and also over the back rail, then underneath again, with about 63 mm ($2\frac{1}{2}$ in.) to spare for finishing. These willows form the warp on which you will weave the seat. On a small chair you will have about seven warp rods on which to weave. When you have completed the warp it is a good plan to tie a piece of thin string from side to side of the chair to hold the warp rods down, otherwise they will stick up in the air until you have done some weaving on them. Have the string right at the front, so that it does not get in the way of your weaving.

To commence the weaving start on the left side of the front rail, and putting the thin end of your first weaver under the left warp rod take it over the next one and then under again and continue over and under across to the right side. (See diagram 40.) Wrap it once round the rail on the right side and then round again and back across the seat going over where you went under on the previous row, and under where you went over. Make a short wrap round the rail on the left side and then go round the rail again and back across the seat. Join the willows as necessary by joining a thick end to a thick end and letting both these ends cross behind one of the warp rods underneath the seat. To join the thin ends, overlap another thin one about 127 mm (5 in.) and work the two along together until the short one is used up. Take each crossing round the side rails, and make an extra wrap round the side rails as necessary to keep the crossing straight. Work right to the back of the seat, closing the rows up as tightly as you can. Leave the last end underneath resting on the warp rod, then thoroughly soak the ends of the warp rods to make them really supple, and take each one in turn over the back rail—underneath the rail and up in the centre of the seat, and then over the first warp rod and leave the end under the next warp rod. (See diagram 41.) It is helpful to pinch these last thick ends with round-nosed pliers to make them bend more easily where they go round the rail. (See photograph 24.)

All the ends underneath can be cut back closely so that they are all resting on a warp rod, but do not cut them until the seat has completely dried out, or they may shrink on to the right side.

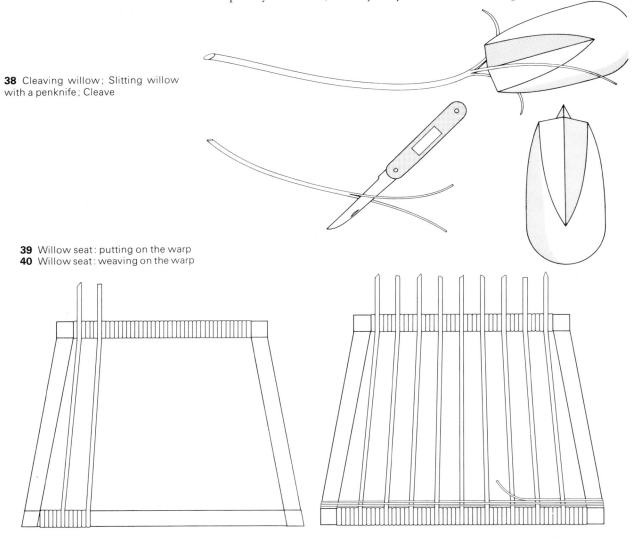

38 Cleaving willow; Slitting willow with a penknife; Cleave

39 Willow seat: putting on the warp
40 Willow seat: weaving on the warp

24 A willow seat

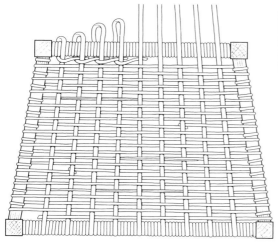

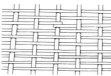

41 Willow seat: finishing detail of weave. Joining willows underneath seat. Thin ends (tips) overlap about 15 cm (6 in.) and work as one. Thick ends (butts) cross each other, resting on a stake

Seating with seagrass

Seagrass is a coarse grass or sedge that grows mainly in China. When harvested it is twisted by machine into a continuous rope. This rope is of varying thicknesses, and can be bought in the natural colour or dyed in many shades of red, blue, brown, green, etc, and it is sometimes available in two colour hanks, ie two different colours twisted together, giving a pleasing effect.

It is a little rough to handle, but is used a great deal for stools, etc as it is very strong. It can be used for check weaving of various kinds, and also in the rush seating pattern.

The seagrass is usually sold in 500 gramme (1 lb) hanks, and at a rough estimate just over a hank will seat a 30 cm (12 in.) square stool. Like rush seats, seagrass and cord also need stools or chairs with raised corners, to hold the weave in place. For a check weave pattern you should work both the top and underneath the seat and so will need two tension sticks—one across the centre on the top of the seat, and one underneath, to keep the tension loose enough to weave the pattern on the warp. Tie these two sticks across the centre of the stool, and you are ready to start. Take a long length of seagrass and wind it on a spool, then tie a single knot at the end and tack this knot inside the frame on the left side rail. Bring the strand from underneath and make one wrap round the front rail and then take it across to the back and make a wrap round the back rail, next to the corner then over the back rail and right round the whole seat twice, so that you have a block of three strands. Now make another short wrap round the front rail, then across and over the back rail, with another short wrap on the back rail between the third and fourth strands. Continue this working right across the stool, and you should have blocks of three strands separated by a short wrap on both the front and back rails. When you reach the end, bring the strand out to the right—under the right side rail and up over it with a short wrap, and then, threading the seagrass into a rush needle, weave over and under each block of three to the left side rail. Make a short wrap on this and then go under the seat and weave the underside strands in the same way. Repeat this row twice more all round the seat making a short wrap on each side rail when the third strand is in place. On the next row of weaving, go under where you went over last time, and over where you went under the blocks of three. Repeat this twice more and after making the short wraps each side, repeat the first row three times.

Your tension sticks can now be removed, and then continue in sequence until the seat is complete. (See photograph 25.) Thread the

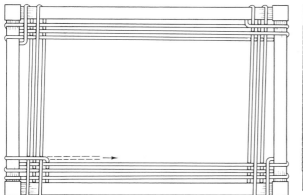

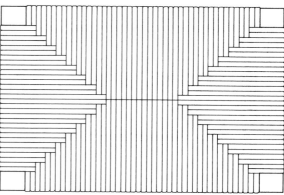

42 Seagrass seat worked with double strands (see text)

43 Completed seagrass seat worked with double strands

25 A seat in seagrass with pattern woven on both sides, making it doubly strong

Old end

New end

44 Joining seagrass by splicing. Un-twist old end to about two or three inches from the end, thread the new piece through, then thread it back again through the old piece for about 25 mm (1 in.) further on. Thread the end of the old piece through the new piece, and pull up together

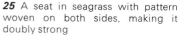

end of the seagrass back through some of the wrappings on the underside of the seat, to finish off. If you wish to weave a different design on the underside of the seat, it is quite in order to do so—the top and underside need not be identical, but the underneath should not be left unwoven.

To join the seagrass untwist the old end about 76 mm (3 in.) from the end and thread the new piece through the twist, then thread it back again about 25 mm (1 in.) further on. Thread the end of the old piece through the new piece, and pull together. This is called 'splicing' and is the correct method of joining. (See diagram 44.) Keep all joins underneath the seat. See whipcord seat photograph 27—pattern can also be used for seagrass.

It is not advisable to use seagrass on metal stools, as metal can cause the seagrass to deteriorate. To use seagrass for the rush pattern seat, tack the knotted seagrass in the front corner of the left side rail, take it over the left side rail—then underneath and across to the right side rail—over it and again underneath and over to the left side rail, underneath again and across and over the right side rail. Now bring it up in the centre of the seat—over the crossings and the front rail, underneath and up over the back rail—again underneath and up over the front rail, then again underneath and over the back rail. Bring the strand up in the centre and over the right side rail at the back—underneath and across over the left side rail—underneath and over the right side rail, and again underneath and over the left side rail. Then bring it up in the centre and over the back rail—underneath and up and over the front rail—again underneath and over the back rail and then up and over the front rail. When working this with seagrass it is advisable to work two strands round each corner instead of one, as the strands, being rather springy, are apt to override each other, but by going round twice they will lie much more evenly. (See diagrams 42 and 43.) This all sounds rather complicated, but if you study the diagrams carefully you will see how it works out. Actually you must go to and fro twice, and then go round the corner to start the next two strands. If the sides are filled in before the back and front rails are filled, finish with a figure of eight movement as shown in the rush seating section. (See whipcord seat photograph 26, also for seagrass.) When it is all completed, finish off by tying the end of the seagrass to a strand opposite on the underside and knot it firmly, tucking the end away.

This seat can also be padded with small pads of paper.

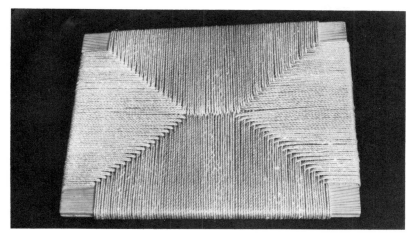

26 Cord seat worked in the rush pattern, but with double strands. Also suitable for seagrass
27 Stool seat in fine cord, woven on both sides, in two colours

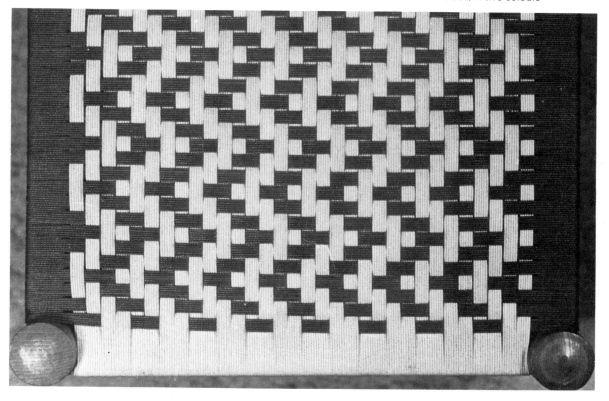

Cord seating

Strictly speaking cord does not come within the specification of 'natural materials', but as it is such a popular medium for stool seating, I am including a short section on it in this book.

The cord used is mostly whipcord, which is very strong and hardwearing, and above all does not stretch. This is a most important point, as some of the materials sold for seating are disappointing because the seats are apt to sag when in use. There are two thicknesses of whipcord mainly used—a fine one which is used for the double seat, ie a seat which is woven on top and also underneath.

A thicker cord is used for the single seats. With all these seats it is helpful to have raised corners on the stools. Also tension sticks are necessary—fairly thin ones for the fine cord, but thicker when using the thick cord. As I have already said in the section on 'close caning' it is almost impossible to give precise sizes for these tension sticks, as everyone works at a different tension, but a stick about 13 mm ($\frac{1}{2}$ in.) wide and 6 mm ($\frac{1}{4}$ in.) thick would be a fairly medium size. If you are apt to knit or embroider very tightly you will probably need a thicker one.

For the double seat lay two sticks across the centre of the stool, one on top of the rails and the other underneath and tie them to the side rails until you have done a few rows to hold them in position. The warp is put on first—make a knot at the end of your ball of cord, and then tack it just inside the left side rail close to the front corner. Bring it up outside the front rail and over it—over the tension stick and the back rail, then underneath, over the tension stick and out at the front again. Continue this wrapping right across the stool, keeping the wraps as close together as possible. When the warp is complete, either bring the cord round the back right side leg of the stool to continue the weaving, or if you are using a different colour, tack it inside the rail as before. Use a needle for the weaving—a smaller version of the rush needle would be suitable—and thread the cord under twelve warp threads and over twelve to the left side rail. On the pattern seat shown there were one hundred and ninety two strands in the warp, which divided up evenly, but try to work so that you have the same number of threads at each end of the row. Work five more rows over and under the same threads as the first row making a block of six rows both on top and underneath the seat. Put a single wrap round each side rail, and then weave over six threads ★ under twelve and over twelve, and repeat from ★ to the end of the row, which should be over six to match the beginning. Work across underneath and then work five more rows over and under the same threads, then start the next block with the short wrap over each rail, and then over twelve threads and under twelve right round the seat again, and repeat this row five times again. Continue with this sequence with a single wrap on each side rail between each block of six rows, and moving the pattern six threads to the left after completing each block. You can continue this pattern right across the seat if you wish, and it makes a pleasing diagonal pattern. If you prefer however, you can reverse the pattern after working four complete blocks, and work three blocks towards the right, and then three blocks towards the left again, continuing this across the seat, giving a chevron effect. (See photograph 27.)

Finish off by threading the end of the cord back under some of the wrappings on the underside, and then knotting it. Any joins you may need to make should be reef knots on the underside, and hidden under the blocks.

A thicker cord should be used for the single seats, and again you will need a tension stick. Put this across the centre of the seat lying on the two side rails, and work the warp over it. Wind about half of the ball of cord into a small ball—knot the end and tack it to the left side rail close to the front corner. Bring it out under the front rail, round the rail once, out into the front and across to the back rail over the tension stick. Make one short wrap round the back rail next to the corner, then bring the cord up in the centre of the seat and make a loop over the first warp thread, down again in the centre and under the back rail—up and over the back rail and through the loop. (See diagram 45.) Bring the cord to the front again and make a loop over the two warp threads on the front rail, then one short wrap before taking the cord over to the back rail again (see diagram 45). Continue this sequence, which gives you two cords through each loop, both back and front, with a short wrap between each pair of cords all the way across the seat. Mark the centre of each side rail with a small pencil mark—bring the cord under the right side rail, and cutting a long length of cord, thread it in the rush needle and start weaving across the warp. Make a short wrap round the right side rail first, and then weave under four cords (two pairs) and over four cords right across the seat—make a short wrap in the corner of the left side rail, and make a loop over this first row, as before—bring the cord up from underneath and over the left side rail, through the loop, and then weave back over and under the same cords as in the previous row. Make the short wrap and the loop again on the right side rail, and then weave the next row over two cords ★ and under four and over four ★ repeating from ★ to ★ right across the seat. Again make the short wrap and the loop, and weave back again under and over the same cords. Continue in this way, being careful to make the loop over each pair of cords, with a short wrap between each pair on both side rails.

Remove the tension stick when you have completed about half the seat, and continue to work in sequence. (See photographs 28 and 49.) To join the cord on the single seat—use long lengths of cord, and when you have used it to within 120–212 cm (4–5 ft) take another long piece and make a single knot at one end, and put this on the inside of the rail underneath, and wrap it in with the short wraps. When you reach the end of the first cord, make a single knot in it, and exchange the two pieces of cord, binding in the old end and continuing the weave with the new piece. The knots will prevent the cords being pulled out, and you will have a strong neat join. (See diagram 47.)

45 Detail of warp for cord seat
28 Single seat in thick cord

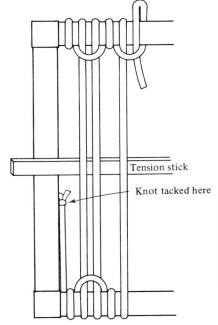

Tension stick

Knot tacked here

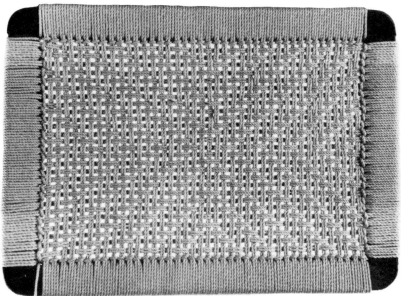

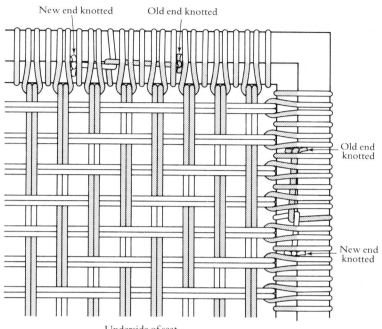

New end knotted   Old end knotted

Old end
knotted

New end
knotted

Underside of seat

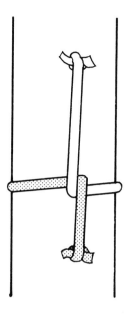

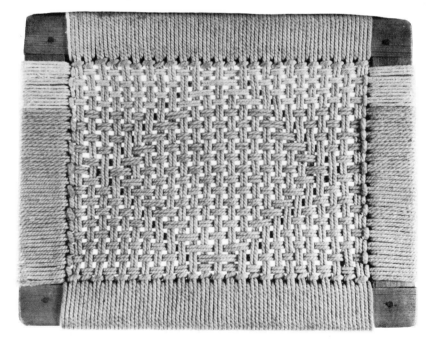

46 Underside of cord seat showing joining of cord

47 Detail showing new and old ends

29 Single seat in thick cord

Special work

30 A decorative chair with seat and back woven with very fine cane, probably French

Photographs 30 to 35 show examples of more complicated work.

31 A pair of nineteenth century English chairs with closely woven seats in very fine cane

32 A small Bentwood chair, showing the method of working the 6 way pattern on a circular seat

33 An ornate magazine rack, probably French, with beautifully caned
sides in the 6 way pattern, using very
fine cane

34 A stool seat in cord with an interesting diamond design

35 An unusual design in very fine
cord

Work chart

Stage 1

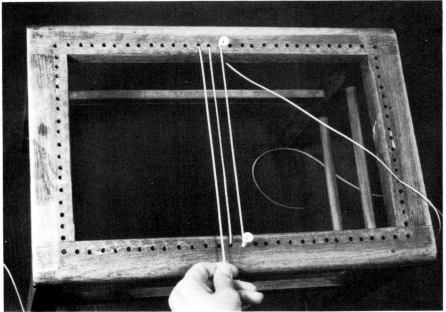

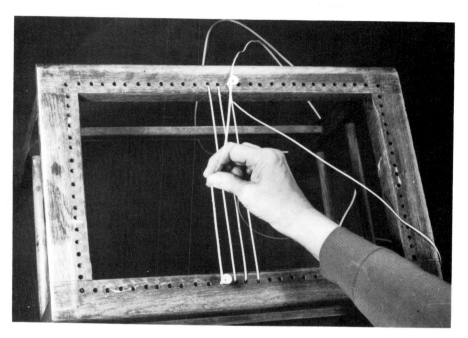

36—41 The six stages which make up
the working chart

Stage 2

Stage 3

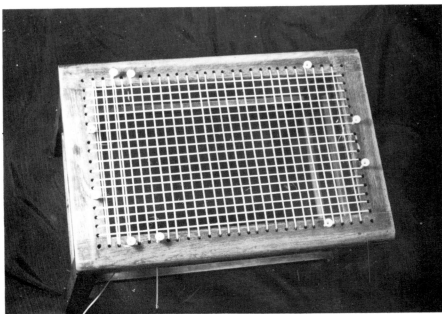

Stage 4

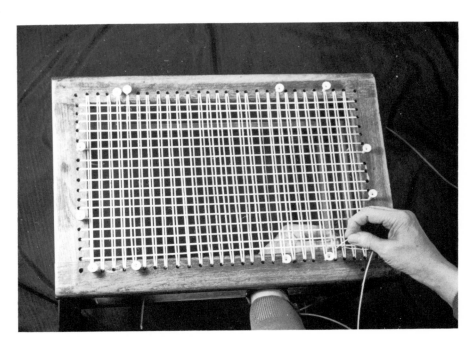

Stage 5

Stage 6

Stage 6   *continued*

Tools

CANE

A small stiletto or bodkin (a sharp pointed tool to lift canes in the later stages of seating)

A clearing tool (a flat topped tool used with a hammer to clear the holes of old cane, etc)

A shell bodkin (a slightly curved tool with a groove in the curve in which cane can be threaded through other canes)

Side cutters or scissors

Flat and round–nosed pliers (sometimes useful to pull canes through the weaving)

Pegs (small pieces of wood, willow or centre cane with which to peg the cane in the holes during seating and also to complete the work)

RUSHWORK

Scissors

Ruler or measure

Rush needle (a large needle, curved and with a large eye. This is easier to use if the curve is cut off, and the needle fitted into a handle. Used for drawing the rushes through when nearing the end of the seating)

Wooden padding stick (used to pad the seat from underneath as the work progresses)

Two small lengths of fine flax string

WILLOW

Side cutters

Penknife and cleave (used for splitting willows)

Glossary

CANE

Chair cane This is the inner bark of the rattan plant—it has a strong glossy surface which is very hard wearing.

Beading The process of covering the holes in the frame with a wider cane, after the seating is completed.

Couching The method of using a narrow cane to hold down the beading cane threaded into every alternate hole.

Thinning When doing the beading there are two wider pieces of cane to go into each corner hole as well as the diagonal weavers, and if they are thinned on the wrong side for about an inch from the end there will be no problem in getting them all into the holes.

CLOSE CANING

Liner A piece of fairly thick centre cane (no. 10 or 12) or palembang brown cane used to line the inside of the seat frame, for the purpose of knotting the close caning over it.

Palembang A brown cane named after a port in Java in which area it grows. Much harder than centre cane, it is used for very strong baskets.

Tension rod A round or flat rod which will reach from side to side of the seat, over which the warp is put on to the seat thus allowing 'play' for the weaving.

RUSHWORK

Bolts Rushes are sold in these bundles which contain rushes of various thicknesses and lengths, usually weighing about 5 to 6 lbs.

Butts Thick end of rush.

Tips Thin end of rush.

WILLOW

Buffing The attractive reddish brown colour is achieved by 'buffing' or boiling the willows—the colour from the bark penetrates the stems thus giving them their colour.

Mellowing After soaking the willows are wrapped tightly in a towel or piece of blanket for several hours or overnight and they will then be ready for use.

SEAGRASS A coarse grass or sedge which grows mainly in the far East.

Splice Method of joining seagrass.

CORD Whipcord is a good material for seating as it is very strong and does not stretch. Some of the modern cords can also be used but care must be taken that they will not stretch or sag.

Short wrap Cord wrapped round the rail itself, and not taken from one side to the other.

Suppliers

GREAT BRITAIN

Chair cane, seagrass and cord

F. Aldous Limited
37 Lever Street
Manchester

Dryad Limited
Northgates
Leicester
also willows and rushes

Jacobs, Young and Westbury
Bridge Road
Haywards Heath
Sussex
also rushes

Smit and Son
99 Walnut Tree Close
Guildford
Surrey
also willows

Growers
Rushes

Tom Metcalfe Arnold
Wildcroft
Holwell
St Ives
Huntingdonshire

Willows

F. E. Hector and Son
Burrowbridge
Bridgewater
Somerset

USA

Naturalcraft
2199 Bancroft Way
Berkeley
California 94704

Cane & Basket Supply Co
1283 South Cochran Avenue
Los Angeles
California 90019

H. H. Perkins Co Inc
10 South Bradley Street
Woodbridge
Connecticut 06525

Triarco Arts & Crafts
7330 North Clark Street
Chicago
Illinois 60626
(write for address of
outlet nearest you)

Newell Workshop
19 Blaine Avenue
Hinsdale
Illinois 60521

Earth Guild/Grateful Union
Mail Order Service
149 Putnam Avenue
Cambridge
Massachusetts 02139

Peerless Rattan & Reed
97 Washington Street
New York
New York 10006

The Workshop
Box 158
Pittsford
New York 14534

Billy Arthur Inc
University Mall
Chapel Hill
North Carolina 27514

Yellow Springs Strings
Box 107
68 Goes Station
Yellow Springs
Ohio 45387

NASCO
901 Janesville Avenue
Fort Atkinson
Wisconsin 53538

Sax Arts & Crafts
Box 2002
Milwaukee
Wisconsin 53201